Listening

❖ ❖ ❖

The Story of the Swan

Several years ago, I noticed that my photos taken on trips always included pictures of swans. I had taken pictures of swans in Russia, Switzerland, England, and Australia, just to name a few places. I asked within why this seemed to be a recurring theme and was reminded of the story of the "Ugly Duckling." You may remember that the "ugly duckling" left his home and hid because he was teased for not being like the other ducks. One day he noticed some beautiful creatures who moved through the water with effortless grace. He wished with all his heart that he could be one of these fantastic birds called swans, instead of a duck—and an ugly one at that. How startled he was upon looking at his reflection to find that he had become a swan while hiding away, and that he had never really been a duck at all.

It's good reminder for all of us. We are truly swans all the time, regardless of what we or others think. We don't have to work to become swans. We just let what is happening naturally occur, and we find to our amazement that we were always swans.

Listening is the way we remember that we are graceful swans when we forget and try to make things hard or painful.

✧   ✧   ✧

Listening

✧ ✧ ✧

*How to Increase Awareness
of Your Inner Guide*

LEE COIT

Published and distributed in the United States By:
Las Brisas Publishing P.O. Box 2987 Ventura, CA. 93002
e-mail info@leecoit.com Phone (805) 208-2805

Edited by Dwayne Copp and Jill Kramer
Designed by Jenny Richards

Quotations from *A Course in Miracles* used by permission of the publisher,
Foundation for Inner Peace, Tiburon, CA

Library of Congress Cataloging-in-Publication Data

Coit, Lee.
    Listening :   how to increase awareness of your inner guide / Lee Coit.
      p.   cm.
    ISBN 1-56170-400-8
    1. Spiritual life. 2. Listening—Religious aspects.   I. Title.
BL624.C633   1996   96-8984
291.4'2—dc20   CIP

ISBN 1-56170-400-8

Twelfth Printing, July 2008

Printed in the United States of America

✧ CONTENTS ✧

Foreword vii
Acknowledgments ix
Introduction xi

Chapter 1: The Secret of the Inner Voice 1

Chapter 2: Beginning to Listen.......................................11

Chapter 3: How Do I Contact My Inner Guide? 21

Chapter 4: Ten Suggestions for Better "Listening" 33

Chapter 5: Seeming Difficulties in "Listening" 55

Chapter 6: Fifteen "Listening" Principles —
        A Checklist 69

Chapter 7: Is It Working? 79

A Closing Note 85
Epilogue 89
Ten Tips for Better "Listening" 91
About the Author 95

(For your convenience, blank pages are placed in the back of this book titled Notes. You may wish to keep track of any insights you receive while reading. This can be your first step in listening. May I also suggest that you consider the value of keeping a daily journal and writing down the guidance you receive on a regular basis.)

✦ FOREWORD ✦

"Listening," long considered by many to be a by-product of Eastern mysticism, has often been dismissed by busy Westerners as highly impractical. It has been thought that the contemplative life, which "listening" supposedly entails, could only be practiced in temples and ashrams. Only those Westerners who have been involved in metaphysical movements and like pursuits have been sympathetic.

In pointing out here that our Source of Truth is as close to us as our own wondering—as close as our own thoughts—Lee Coit takes the mystery out of "listening," and the Divine within each of us becomes recognizable. In providing criteria for the recognition of our own holiness, he helps us to bypass the "static" and the babble that buzz through our busy minds.

Fantastic as this may seem, it works. I have been closely involved with Lee in numerous projects in the past two years, from a Forgiveness Day celebration led by him in the Anaheim Convention Center, in Anaheim, California, to several conferences, and on to the planning and building of a Retreat Center in Riverside County, California, to name just a few. His has always been the guiding hand on the helm, the inspiration, the calming influence. His "listening" to the Spirit within has become an example to all who know him.

He lives it in his daily life. His courage, spiritual strength, imagination, creativity, and faith have been inspiring to all of us who have come to value his friendship.

We have been encouraged to "listen" in our own right, partly as a result of his influence, and have uncovered our own "inner voices." To be sure, most of us already were listening, pursuant to our study of *A Course in Miracles*, but have been encouraged and inspired by Lee to continue, as we have shared our "revelations"—in music, poetry, prose, artistic expression, and in our daily living.

All of us can use the methods and practices described in this booklet. We can learn how to identify, and how to listen to, our loving "inner voice," as well as how to bypass our judgmental side. We can learn how to tap the source of the joy that is waiting within us. We can use the checklist to monitor our "listening," as well as the ten suggestions to "go within." None of these require lengthy periods of contemplation, but can be experienced as we work, drive, walk, eat, or meditate. Our "inner voice" is always broadcasting.

Happy listening!

—Dwayne Copp, Editor

✧ ✧ ✧

✧ ACKNOWLEDGMENTS ✧

This book is dedicated to my friends—to all the people who have been supportive and loving throughout my life. As my awareness of my inner guide increases, so does my appreciation of my friends, who often serve as embodiments of this guidance. This book was made possible by those friends, who are like a family to me.

I would like to acknowledge two of these friends, Dwayne and Alma Copp, who gave me encouragement and support, as well as hours and hours of editing and rewriting. They brought my unorganized notes to a cohesive form. There is not enough space to name all the others, so I will thank all of you at once, until I can thank each of you personally, knowing that you will understand.

✧   ✧   ✧

✧ ✧ ✧

Open your mind to the part of your being that is constantly in touch with your highest expression.

✧ INTRODUCTION ✧

Dear Reader:

It's been many years since *Listening* was first published. Since the beginning, this book has been a vehicle to share a wonderful discovery—my inner voice. This discovery has helped me find inner peace, happiness, and contentment. Until I became aware of this presence in my life, my existence seemed to be made up of disjointed experiences. With the clarity given me through inner guidance, I began to see the overall pattern—not only in my life—but in the lives of all the people who came into my awareness. In the beginning, so that I could concentrate on this inner search, I sold my business and stopped all other activity. My search has now covered a 20-year span, and I have come full circle. I have been to the mountaintop.

I have spent many years releasing my self-limiting concepts and increasing my awareness of Truth. I have returned to a more ordinary life, but I now view it from an extraordinary perspective. I am not sure you have to take such drastic measures. It is my hope that by sharing what I have learned, I may be able to save you some stress and time. However, the journey is an individual one, and each soul must undertake and complete it alone.

What started as a small effort to share my discovery in a few self-published books has now reached well over 200,000 copies and publication in eight languages. My desire to share with a few others who might be having similar experiences with this fantastic source of guidance has grown to a circle of thousand of friends around the world. How blessed this journey has been. The full story is contained in my three books: Listening, Accepting, and Being. For over twenty years my spiritual journey has covered the world and included joy and sorrow, quiet and confusion, activity and repose. At times I have been asked to sacrifice nearly all I held dear and yearned for, only to find that what I lost I really did not want after all. Strange to say I have learned not knowing is just fine.

The Search Begins

Following their inner voice has changed the life of thousands of my friends. I know it will change your life if you choose to "listen." In the beginning, my search did not begin by following a spiritual path. In fact, I thought my early spiritual training was part of my problem, and I was seeking to free myself from it. I was unable to reconcile what I had been taught as a child about God and living a good life with my actual experiences as an adult, which were that selfishness and greed often seemed to win. My search was simply trying to find out whether life makes sense, has a logical sequence, and follows a set of principles, or is it simply chaotic. Frankly, I thought it was more likely that it was just a series of random incidents. It appeared possible that we humans attempted to place occurrences in a meaningful sequence because we were unable to deal with the idea that life might not be beneficent. Maybe we feared that creation was not orderly, but merely a series of random accidents. Were we all doomed to oblivion by cruel, whimsical fate? It seemed very important in 1979 for me to find the answer to this puzzle.

My Big Question: "Does Life Make Sense?"

I knew the answer had to be one of these two possibilities: Either our lives are governed by principle, or life is a random selection of events with no governing purpose. There is no compromise possible between order and chaos or between principle and accident. One accident in an orderly string of events is still chaos. Consistency can have no exception. So I determined to conduct a grand experiment. I would find out whether life had meaning and order or if it was chaotic. But how would I do this? I decided that if life had order, there must be a governing principle or set of principles. I knew that many people had tried to find them, and yet I had never heard an answer that satisfied me. I started with the assumption that there was order and a governing principle. I decided to use an old technique that worked for me when I was in the advertising business. I would then simply wait for the principle if it was all-powerful to become evident. I set a time limit on this experiment and decided to devote one full year to it. It may seem crazy now, but at the time it was the best I could do. I had moved near the beach, and I decided to run to the ocean each morning after meditation and sit there for an hour or so and wait for my answer. I also decided to devote the rest of the day and night to being alert for any clues that might come to me.

I figured out that if this principle that I called God did not appear in one year, either it did not care or it was not so all-powerful. Failure would be fine; I just wanted to know if there was anything out there. Without knowing it, I had taken the first step necessary in finding my inner guide and that was to be still and wait for the answers to come. In a month or so, things began to happen. Little books came into my life. Sometimes the messages were on television or on the radio, and sometimes they were just thoughts I had while sitting on my rock by the ocean. I became aware of a pattern to the information I was getting and became conscious that something was beginning to "teach" me in a logical sequence.

Over the next year, these sequences of "lessons" continued to grow, and as I experimented with the information, I started getting amazing results. Eventually I took a seven-month trip to Europe and used my inner guide to make every decision. This was a perfect place for my experiment because I was now in an environment that was totally strange to me. Now my own knowledge was valuable, and that made *"listening"* easier. When I returned, I became involved with a group of people studying *A Course in Miracles,* and from that group a number of us started the Las Brisas Retreat Center. It was at this Center on a mountain in Southern California that the information for this book first came though. This happened in a most interesting way, as you will read below.

How *"Listening"* Came About

When I returned from Europe, I decided to share my slides privately with a friend and his family at an *A Course in Miracles* convention. It was the first such event I had ever attended, so I just wanted to sit back and see what was happening. It was all very new to me, and even though the material was easy for me to assimilate on my own, I had no idea what others were doing with it. That evening, to my complete surprise, I was asked to show my slides to the entire group. They wanted to know how I had followed my inner guide during my travels. I was in shock, and mad at my inner guide, who I knew had set this whole thing up. The story of my travels was not always pretty or even spiritual. There was a lot of loss and struggle, as much of what happened as a result of listening to inner guidance was that I had to give up my most cherished beliefs. I was unwilling to talk about this search for inner guidance because it was very personal, and I was still unsure what I was doing and how inner guidance worked. Despite my fears at being thought weird, I told these strangers the truth about my adventures. To my surprise, everyone seemed to enjoy my stories very much. Instead of being an outcast, as I had feared, I made many close friends, and I had one of the most pleasant weekends of my life.

The Sharing Begins

Some of these people asked me to travel to other meetings at various locations on the West Coast and share my story. My travels increased as more people asked me to share. Mostly I just showed my slides, played music, and told what little I knew. I was often asked how I contacted my inner guide, but I really could not verbalize what happened. For the most part, all I did was to wait and be quiet. Then, sometimes this marvelous information just came to me. There were so many requests for information on how to do *"listening"* that I finally asked my inner guide what I should share. It was then that I was given the ten tips you will find in the back of this book. I handed these out for free at every lecture I gave. That was all I got for several months until my inner guide told me to do a meditative weekend at the site of the new Retreat Center. I was to read lessons from *A Course in Miracles* that my guide assigned at the beginning of each hour and then meditate for the rest of the hour. I was to do this each hour for two days from 8:00 in the morning until 5:00 in the evening. Several people who were involved in the Retreat Center asked if they could join me.

Each hour when I meditated, after reading the assigned lesson, I got bombarded with information on inner guidance. I was typing it as fast as I could and not doing a very good job. When Dwayne Copp saw what I was typing, he asked if he could read the material. He liked it, and at the end of the weekend he told me that he would put it in a better form. He had just bought a new computer and said he needed to practice on it. It was Dwayne's encouragement that brought this material into book form. When he was done, I took his typed copy of this book to a Quick Print Shop and printed 500 copies, using all the money I had in the bank. I was told to save all the money from the books that were now sold after each slide show. That turned out to be good advice, for I needed it to print up the next batch of books. For about a year, the book continued in a very simple form until Stephen Swartz, a New York printer who became a very inspirational writer, offered to put the book in a better format. After that, several distributors discovered the book, as well as some foreign publishers. No one was ever solicited to promote this work. The last ten years have been an amazing story of spectacular growth in distribution without any sales effort on my part.

As I write the introduction for this revised edition, there are very few changes I want to make to the original manuscript. Not only has it been most accurate, just as it was given to me, but it contains material that is only now fully understandable to me. For example, in the old introduction, I wrote "inner guide, which is an integral part of my being." Little did I know that I would write three books in a series at that point and that the final book, *Being,* would be devoted to how my inner guide is actually my real Self. My second book, *Accepting,* started to emerge shortly after I finished *Listening.* The importance of accepting is discussed several times in this first book even though I was unaware of the process at that time. *Accepting* covers using *"listening"*—not only to get answers to questions, but to see things clearly, thereby finding inner peace. What is so wonderful about what happened and what it has become is that when we "listen," we are given the complete picture even if we are unaware of it.

Limited vs. Fearful

Here are the few changes I would make after all this time. The first one is to clarify your awareness of how the ego works. In the beginning, I viewed my ego as something that had gotten me into a lot of trouble. I was very devoted to finding a better way to live. I wanted to stop being guided by my fearful and selfish reactions. During the past 20 years, I have seen how well inner guidance works, and now I take a more gentle view of my ego. I see it as something that has never really worked, no matter how hard it tried. As my inner guide told me, "Don't hate your ego. It is the only thing in the universe that doesn't know where it is, doesn't know what it is, and self-destructs when left alone. Just look on its efforts with love, and leave it alone."

I no longer see my ego as fear based even though at times it is very fearful. A better description of my ego is "limited." My first voice or ego gives me a "limited" concept of who I am and what creation is. It is trying to help and protect me, but it does not know who I really am or what creation really is. Its perspective is strictly limited to how things affect me. When our egos combine, they seem to have power and seem to be able to create a universe in which both love and hate, truth and falsity, and life and death are possible. This is an illusion that has no power except the power we give it. It can be easily walked through without effect by anyone who follows inner guidance and "listens."

The Limited Voice

Second, when I want to tell the difference between the two voices, I simply *"listen"* carefully to what they are each saying. If one voice sees me, others, or the situation as limited, I know it's my ego. For example, "There's only so many left, so we'd better hurry" is a voice speaking whose view of the situation is based on a limited idea of supply. My real inner guide sees me, others, and the situation as unlimited. It says, "You have plenty of time, and there is enough for everyone." It sees everyone as inner connected, with no one taking from anyone else. Rather than avoid your ego voice, it is important to listen to it carefully; the content of the message will tell you which voice is your inner guide and which is your ego.

Third, my inner voice's guidance includes me and also everyone involved in the situation. It sees our connection as real and constant. What I hear blesses me, but it also blesses everyone. Sometimes inner guidance moves slower than I think it should to give everyone time to become willing to participate. Sometimes when I *"listen"* to my inner guide, I am told to give to someone else, and sometimes I am told to receive. I must not let my perception of what is "right" interfere with this guidance. Thus, I must expand my idea of my unlimited self in order to remain in tune with inner guidance. I cannot just ask for what will benefit me. I must ask for and be willing to accept what benefits everyone involved in the situation and see us all as One.

Finally, I want to stress that inner guidance is very individual. Some hear an actual voice, others see pictures or colors, others get bodily feelings, and others get combinations of all of these. No way is superior. Try to develop what is most natural for you. For some people, the inner guide comes as the first voice that speaks, and the ego is the second voice. For me, I hear my inner guide second, or maybe it is the only voice I hear. Since inner guidance is individual, it will come in the form most easy for you to accept and understand.

This book will acquaint you with the wonderful fact that we can find answers to all our questions. The source of this information is within our being and within our real minds. The source of this knowledge is far beyond our own conscious thinking ability, but not beyond our unlimited *"being."*

Let me acquaint you with the methods and steps that will enable you to find your inner guide and to embark on your own path to the discovery of your true nature and the attainment of inner peace and contentment. These are just guidelines. I have put them forth as they work for me. I have tried to use personal examples where they will help. If your path does not exactly match mine, that is fine. We are all going in the same direction.

Many of the examples that I've used occurred during my seven-month journey to Europe during the early 1980s. It was then that I first put all my decisions in the hands of my inner guide. My purpose was to watch and see what would happen when I relied entirely on this inner guidance. Having used this type of intuitive thinking during my 20 years in the advertising business, I wanted to put it to the ultimate test— a minute-by-minute, total dependence experiment. I did this, and the results were truly astonishing. My needs were taken care of in ways I never could have planned.

I discovered that what I had used before only on special occasions, times when there seemed to be no other choice, worked not only for major decisions, but for the most minute ones. I had found a new source of knowledge—it was located within me beyond my conscious mind, but was easily accessible for constant use.

This may seem impossible to you now, but let me assure you that my life during the last 20 years has been a daily testimony that this is true. Logic cannot explain it, but if you will use the methods described in this book, your experience will show you that it can be done. If you do this with devotion, I can assure you that your life will be transformed into something more beautiful than you can ever imagine.

If your present "problem-solving" methods do not work in a completely satisfying way, read on and learn how to contact your own inner guide.

✧ ✧ ✧

Your true potential is as close as your inner thoughts and as bright as the most creative insight. This exists in all of us, and when it finds expression, it is called genius!

◇ ◇ ◇

*The only requirement for
hearing your inner guide is your
willingness. Openness to direction is
required for guidance. If you
are not aware of guidance,
you do not desire it.*

CHAPTER 1

The Secret of the Inner Voice

There is a power in us that is of God. It gives us strength, vision, success, and peace. We all use this power to some degree; no one can totally lose it, yet few realize its full potential. This power is reached in a most unusual way—by "going inside" ourselves. Many have searched for it in countless ways, but few have found it because it is hidden where most never look—"inside." We can reach it quite simply by just letting go of all the babble and churning within our minds—reaching below this noisy level to the peace and strength that constantly abides in us. From the time we were little children, we have been trained to look outside ourselves for answers—in our parents and in the world around us. We can train ourselves to look within.

This inner strength is often reached only in times of crisis. Then we realize that we can, of ourselves, do nothing except turn over our problems to a higher power. As long as we are trying to find solutions with our own strength, determination, and intelligence, we are not successful on a permanent basis. We go from problem to problem, thinking that *this* time we will be able to find the answer. Yet the answer never comes, so we repeat our mistakes over and over in new ways. Finding our inner strength is quite simple in terms of how to do it, but it "seems" to take great effort to do it consistently.

To reach our inner voice, we must give up our attempts to solve problems with our own conscious, intellectual, busy minds. We need to give up the belief that we know what has to be done. We must be open to all possibilities and resort to the strength and wisdom deep within us. This can be done by a trained mind in an instant, with no special preparation, but an untrained mind may find this simple task quite difficult and even threatening. The process of "inner listening" is not mystical, magical, or even difficult, although to the uninitiated it may seem that way. Just three simple steps are needed to train our minds properly.

The Three Steps

The **first step** is to realize that we cannot solve, or even identify, our problems with our "worldly" mind—the conscious mind that we often identify as being us.

Second, we must know that we have the power within us to solve the problem, and that we can strengthen this belief to the point where we are willing to let go of all our "worldly" efforts to find a solution and be guided only by our "inner voice."

And **third,** we must take the final step: Do it. We must calm our conscious mind of all its busy worry, all its attempts to find a solution, and go deep within—beyond this noise—to the quiet and peace that is inside of us. This can take the form of meditation, using all types of tools such as being in a quiet place, assuming special bodily positions, or utilizing special items such as incense and candles. But these forms are not necessary. We need to reach the calm and peace within us, giving up our conscious attempts only for an instant. A trained mind can do this in any situation in the blink of an eye. Our minds become trained by our willingness to turn inside on every possible occasion.

We recognize that we are successful when we feel a sense of peace and power coming over us. We are now in contact with our inner guide. We begin to realize that we are taken care of in all things, and we will be told if and when actions are necessary. Our purpose for attaining this sense of peace is not to be told to do something, but to realize that we are safe, cared for, and at peace. We are always in touch with God's strength, the power of all creation, the order of all things—the principle that governs in peace and harmony. When we know this, a problem no longer exists. We then realize that the "problem" is not a problem, and that we can proceed in strength, confidence, and peace. If something needs to be done by us, we will be told what to do. If we need something, it will be sent to us. Now we can proceed calmly. We need not hurry, search, or change things. We can step back and be guided and cared for.

Withholding Judgment and Choosing to Listen Inside

My seven-month stay in Europe turned out to be a "laboratory," where the three steps discussed before were discovered.

Of my many European experiences, one comes to mind as I write this. I was driving in France on a beautiful, sunny afternoon. My car was very much underpowered, so I had chosen not to drive on the expressways, but to stay on the scenic back roads, which were more to my taste, anyway. However, on this particular day, it did not seem wise to travel the back roads, since the car was overheating and in need of a special part. But then I realized that my fear was about to cause me to miss some beautiful sights, and I decided— "wise" or not—to continue on my way. I halfway expected to have to spend the night in some farmer's field, possibly being rousted as a trespasser. My inner voice assured me that I was okay and all would work out fine, but I was still not totally relieved.

The car continued to heat up, and I proceeded to play with the fan belt adjustment that was causing the problem, which could not be repaired without a special, hard-to-get part. Since it was Sunday, I knew it was useless to look for a mechanic. Everyone had told me about Frenchmen and their disinterested ways, and I believed it to be true. Even on weekdays, during working hours, and in a big city, it was difficult to get help. Parts for my Czechoslovakian car were not easy to get, even in Paris. In the country, and on Sunday, it would be impossible. My prejudgment of Frenchmen tended to be confirmed. Earlier I had tried several service stations where the proprietors just shook their heads. However, I hoped for the best and continued to enjoy my trip. I felt a little worried, but I went on.

After a while, I spotted a garage ahead with an open door.

It was not the first garage I had seen, nor the first at which I had stopped. However, I heard from my inner voice to stop, and so I did. (This was no heavy-handed command, but a gentle suggestion that I should try one more time to get help.) The family was eating on the patio above the garage, and the man motioned to me to come up. I explained my plight in very poor French mixed with English, using what I thought was a French accent. He nodded and offered me wine and bread. No help for the car, but who turns down country bread and wine served on a sunny patio in the south of France?

After a delightful repast, the man proceeded to find the necessary parts for my Czechoslovakian car in a huge parts room in his dingy warehouse. I still don't know why he had all those parts in such a small country garage! He worked for almost an hour to get it just right, although at that point I would have settled for much less. And after all that, the man would not take one franc for his efforts and kindnesses, despite my offers.

An isolated case? No. This type of thing happened in a radiator shop in Switzerland, as well as in an electrician's shop in Austria, where I was charged only five dollars for several hours' work by a former World War II prisoner-of-war who had been interned in Colorado. On many other occasions, people went out of their way to help—for no apparent reason except love.

Who am I to judge? At this date, I cannot even judge those who could not, or would not, help. I simply do not know all the facts. What I am saying is that the less we prejudge and the less we are sure of what the outcome of any situation will be, the more open we are to an acceptance of what happens. The more we trust, the more wonderful experiences we will have, and the better we will be able to follow our inner guide.

The basis for "listening," therefore, is our willingness to "go inside" and to choose to listen by dropping our prejudgment, being quiet, and knowing in our "hearts" that the process will work. We are being cared for at all times, despite what we think is happening.

Inner Knowledge Is Available to Us

It is important to be aware that we all hear essentially the same message, although each of us may hear it in a different form. It is also true that the whole body of *knowledge—yes, I am convinced, the totality of all knowledge*—is available for each of us to draw upon if we expand our efforts to listen. However, we have trained ourselves not to "go inside" and "listen." The reason that this is true is another story, and not relevant to our present discussion of learning to "listen." That this involves fear of knowing our true nature and of reaching our full potential is all we need to realize in order to start being aware of our inner guide.[1] Therefore, to hear the truth, we must be willing to *know* it.

Where Do We Find Answers?

The simple fact is that our answers come in all forms. Help is everywhere. When we quiet ourselves, put our "busy problem solver" away, go inside and open our minds—when we are at peace—the answer comes in a myriad of forms. It is in music, painting, poetry, in our loving friends, our "enemies," and strangers—everywhere we are willing to look. It can be found on billboards, in jokes, in quiet, in trees, in oceans, and in streams. The truth is that our "friend," our inner voice, is with us everywhere we go. But we can only hear it and see it when we are willing. Thus, the secret of hearing is a willingness to "listen" to our inner guide no matter what form the answer takes. Inner-guide answers can come in the form of ideas or from outside reminders that trigger our minds. I often get answers in the form of a

---

[1] See partial discussion in *"Our Split Minds Seem Real,"* in Chapter 5 of this book. The books that make up *A Course in Miracles* give a full discussion of the "fear of knowing." Refer to text pages 225-228.

reminder—a seemingly unrelated thought or occurrence that puts the pieces of the puzzle together.

The particular form or medium in which we hear our "voice" may be determined by our background, education, current interests, or the talents we have. Those who like to write, for example, may hear their voice best with pen in hand or at the typewriter. Others hear best while they are running, hiking, reading, painting, building, meditating, or listening to or playing music. In one form or another, the inner voice is always there, as close as our next thought.

To illustrate this point, suppose we consider ourselves bombarded by thousands of messages every moment, all saying the same thing, but in different forms. Also, consider that we have set our reception device on "off." To receive messages, we must first turn it on. Next, we can choose any channel, and we will get the message in the form of that broadcast. However, we must be able to accept the fact that the answer is contained in that form. Its relevance to our problem merely depends on our willingness to accept the answer as it comes. We can find answers everywhere. The selection is endless. At first, this seems to be an overstatement, but be assured that after we initially accept the answer in one form, we will see it repeated over and over in other forms until we wonder how we could have ever missed it in the first place.

Our inner voice is talking to us all the time, but we only hear it when we really want to! The awareness of our voice's presence is our responsibility. We can't pick up the message on our receiver until we turn it on, tune it in, and "listen." Despite the fact that the broadcast is constantly being beamed to us, we must "want" to listen.

❖ ❖ ❖

CHAPTER 2

Beginning to "Listen"

Those in the beginning stages of listening often report hearing two or more "voices." Inner voices are not any different from those we hear when we talk to ourselves—a sort of inner dialogue. And we *do* talk to ourselves, whether we are aware of it or not. If we have ever wondered about an idea or a current event or wondered why something exists—that wondering in our mind is our "voice." It is not thunderous, raucous, or even quiet. It's just our "voice." It may take on certain special characteristics if it will assist the listener.

"Why?" we ask ourselves.

Aha! See, we do talk to ourselves! This is one way the truth comes to us—in the form of our own thoughts—the form that we can accept the easiest. Simply because it is always with us, waiting to be heard, we cannot miss it unless we so choose.

We Seem to Hear Two Voices

Since we are used to talking to ourselves, taking both sides of an internal conversation, we seem to hear two voices. We seem to have split our minds into two parts. When we ask ourselves what to do about this or that, the answer that we hear is our "voice" speaking. We need not expect the "voice" or "voices" we hear to be very much different from our own wondering.

There are some differences, however, and it is helpful to recognize them. Our daily, busy minds see much to do and create many needs to be filled. However, our contemplative side sees order, joy, and harmony. This creative, intuitive mind enjoys beauty and peace. As long as we feel in conflict, the experience of these two voices will continue. The one is prejudging and limited, the other insightful and unlimited. "Prejudgment," as used here, is not the same as logic, but may include logic. As we become more aware of our "insight" or "inner guide," the first voice, our "prejudgment," becomes less dominant and more quiet. The less importance we give its tendency to judge in advance, the more we seek to remain open-minded, and the sooner this first voice will recede. Keeping our mental slate clean, being open to the answer in any form, and dropping our prejudices and prejudgments all help to reduce the experience of multiple voices.

It's good to become an observer of our thoughts—to see which thoughts are based on prejudgment, fear, prejudice, and lack of trust—and which thoughts are trusting, open, loving, and peaceful. If we dig deeply and honestly enough, we will find that all thoughts are from one of these two sources.

If we find that our mind is preoccupied with things that need to be done, it helps to make a list as they occur, until all these "busy" thoughts subside. Then, with our mind calm, we can "go inside" to "listen." When we are finished "listening," we can then return to the list we have made. We may find that few of these things really need our attention. I even make a list while I "listen" so that my fear of forgetting something important is reduced. Then, when I finish my quiet time, I review the list and do the things that still seem important in the order of their seeming urgency. Often, I find that few of my listed items need to be done now, and that their order of importance has changed. "Listening" gives perspective to our lives.

Examples of My Experience with These Two Voices

I was recently reviewing some of my notes from several years ago, written when I was struggling hard to improve my "listening." Having devoted the first month of my stay in Europe to total "listening," I had progressed only far enough to have a pretty good insight and to hear suggestions and ideas that I didn't think came from my conscious, problem-solving mind. I had not yet gotten to a stage where I could ask my inner voice questions and then get answers that I felt were reliable.

As I worked on this more and more, trying to hear, asking about everything, and learning to ask questions without any investment in the answers, I became aware that at times I would hear two voices, one not agreeing with the other. I watched to see how these two voices worked. The pattern was fairly consistent.

The First Voice

The "first" voice always answered quickly with suggestions for things to do and much to think about. It would, if I followed it, send me here and there and bring up lots of possibilities. While the first voice seemed certain of what I should do, I noticed that it usually was rapid, forceful, worried, and often fearful (limited). For example, if I asked whether I was late for an event, it would suggest that I take shortcuts, drive faster, and not stop to pick up hitchhikers. As long as I "listened" to the "first" voice, I never had a feeling of peace or real confidence, yet I did feel that I was contacting something beyond my intellectual reasoning—some type of inner knowledge.

It's easy to describe this now, but at the time, this voice could convince me that it was right and that I needed to do something immediately. As I looked more closely at what it wanted me to do, I could see that the basis for its decisions was often fear (limitation)—fear of missing out, fear of being late, or fear of all types of things. As I thought about it, this negativity did not seem to be the type of advice I would get from a peaceful and all-knowing source.

You may say here, "Of course not! How could he have been fooled for an instant?"

But I will assure you that the voice sounded factual, logical, concerned about my welfare, and often very much in agreement with my own "rational" evaluation of the situation.

Example A

For instance, while waiting in the customs line at the

Swedish border, I continued to get pushed to the back by crowds of arriving tourists. The attendants made no attempt to organize the line, and with all the crowding, after about 30 minutes I was no closer to getting my passport stamped than I was when I came in the door. I asked inside about what to do and was quickly reminded that I was getting pushed back and that these rude people would continue to do so unless I asserted myself in the same manner that they were doing.

Fortunately, for my peace of mind, I had learned gradually that this first voice was not always the one to "listen" to, and I calmly waited for a second voice. I don't remember exactly what I heard, but I was assured that I would be taken care of and that I should love everyone in the place, from those crowding in, to the seemingly uncaring attendants. I went outside, took some pictures of the beautiful scenery, and returned, not worried about waiting. In a very short time, I was at the front of what I laughingly called a line, and was taken care of while many others around me became angry about the confusion.

Example B

This same thing happened in Yugoslavia during an acute fuel shortage that covered a large area in the southern part of that country. The gas lines were several miles long, and people would often wait in them all day—and still get no gas. I heard clearly from my second voice not to fear, but to keep driving, even though I was low on gas, had not seen a service station for miles, and had not seen any at all for two days that didn't have huge lines.

As the car loped along, I had a wonderful experience involving a boy who was herding sheep along the road. It was not unusual for me to see people herding animals, but this boy stood out at the time, and even more so in retrospect. He waved as I drove toward him, and I waved back. We waved and waved until I drove out of sight over the top of a long hill. I remembered how much as a boy I had longed to travel and had read for hours of Richard Halliburton and his travels around the world. I knew from the boy's reaction to my strange car, with all the stickers from foreign countries, that he was fascinated by this traveler, and so it was now my turn to share a boy's dream. This time, I was the traveler.

I wrote a poem that evening about the shepherd boy and of the wonders of traveling with a turned-on imagination, hoping that our brief encounter had encouraged him to travel someday, as I, too, had been encouraged by R.H. and his fantastic adventures. I stopped worrying about the gas lines. I felt at peace and that I was right where I belonged. I knew all was well and that I need not worry about a gas shortage stranding me in the middle of nowhere—despite the stories I heard that night in the campground from other travelers.

The next day, after this wonderful experience, I saw a gas station with fewer than 20 cars in line. Believe me, that truly seemed like a miracle! Even though the limit I could buy would probably be only ten liters, I pulled in. Any amount of gas would help, although I needed 20 liters to get to Greece, and this was the only station I had seen open in the last two days. The day was hot, and we all pushed our cars by hand closer and closer to the pumps. When I was one car from the pump, up drove an official-looking vehicle, and the station operator and the officers in the car got into a heated argument. Although I didn't understand what the man, the officials, or the crowd were shouting about, I knew that the station was being shut down and that I was just one car away. Oh, no, what should I do? This was my last chance to get gas! My "first" voice and I were very worried.

My second voice, however, told me to be patient and keep going. The car in front finished, and the argument between the attendant and the officials still continued. There were two lines, and as the car across from me was being pushed forward to its pump, I did the same with mine. I took the nozzle in my hands and started to fill my tank, expecting to be stopped at any moment. The argument continued, and I filled the entire tank, with no one telling me to stop at the normal ten-liter limit. I paid the attendant, and as the official clamped the lock on the pump, I drove away. Both experiences seemed dreamlike in that I was suddenly lifted away from the confusion and the anger around me and was able to feel peaceful and loving. And why not feel peaceful? I was being taken care of.

These are just two small examples of the care I have received daily in my life, both in Europe and since then. When I "listen," and then feel the calm and the love in my heart that "listening" shows me, I *know* (not *wish*, but *know*) that I will be taken care of, and I am. I am at peace in a miraculous way, willing to accept what is happening around me. Being taken care of, I do not have to change anything or try to protect myself or provide for my needs.

I do not pretend to know how all this works, and my logical mind cannot explain it. Of course, just loving, or trying to love people, is not the whole answer. My loving is not enough; I must ask my guide what to do, what is happening, and how to see it.

But my faith that I will be taken care of, coupled with "listening" to my inner voice for direction and assurance, does have the power to make me feel peaceful and protected and to experience this harmony. This peacefulness is not a feeling of resignation—that what will happen will happen—but confidence that what is happening is for the best, no matter what my own "judgment" or my "first voice" may tell me.

The Second Voice—The True Guide

How do we get in touch with this second voice? I am not certain that everyone "hears" these two voices. However, since many have reported similar experiences, I assume that it happens fairly often. This second voice has been called the still, small voice, the Voice for God, the inner guide, the Christ vision, the Holy Spirit, intuition, and many other names. But by whatever name it is called, it is available to all of us for direction and reassurance. Its use requires our desire to seek help from within, as well as our willingness to be quiet and listen.

✧ ✧ ✧

CHAPTER 3

How Do I Contact My Inner Guide?

At the beginning of my European trip, I decided to turn over all decisions, large and small, to my inner guide— where I stayed, when and what I ate, the kind of car I bought, and where to visit. I made no plans and had no prior arrangements with anyone. I gave the experiment six months. I watched my mind to see how it worked, how it would decide on things, and how it reacted to what it experienced. When I got a suggestion, answer, feeling, or thought, I examined it to see what its basis was, and, therefore, where it came from. In the beginning, I had the experience of two voices, and so it became a process of looking at each message I'd receive, identifying where it came from, and then deciding what to do—that is, ignore or act—depending on the source.

Here's an example of how it would happen: When deciding what to do about finding a campsite for the evening, I would ask, "Is this the one?"

Often the answer came right away: "Yes. Stop at this campground. This is a good one."

I could see that it was a good campsite, indeed, but that was not enough. Was it the right one? I would often wait and ask again, "Should I stop here?" The second voice would be experienced at speaking more slowly and at not giving instructions. It would say (or more accurately, I would have an inner feeling, which is what it usually is), "Why do you want to stop here?"

I would answer, "Because this campsite is nice, and I am afraid that I won't find another."

Then the thought would come: "Afraid...is my decision based on fear (limitation)? What do I really want? Do I really want to drive a few hours more? Am I tired? Am I hungry? Is this really where I want to stop? What is my real reason for wanting to stop here? Fear? Peace? Compromise? Limitation?

Fear (Limitation)— The Basis for the First Voice

In the beginning, I was not always sure whether the first or the second voice was speaking, but the process was clear—my main reason for listening to the initial advice to stop was my fear that this was the only campsite around. It was my experience in the beginning steps of "listening" that the first voice I heard was based on fear (limitation). But don't use my experience as the only rule. Be aware, and examine the basis for your decisions. Do the answers come from a feeling of calm, well-being, and harmony, or do they come from fear that you are not being cared for?

Peace—The Basis for the Second Voice

When I finally decided that fear (limitation) would not be the basis for my decisions, and went on, the second voice would say, "You will now find a better place." And I always did. Always! I used this technique to find all types of things—to decide which road to take, how to get through confusing towns, where and when to eat, where to exchange money, where to find telephones, and to make literally every type of decision. During the seven-month stay (I had planned six months but stayed seven—so much for that plan!), few

decisions were made without consulting my inner voices—
first number one, and then number two. After a while, the
first voice was quiet most of the time, and number two was
more evident. And so number one became relegated to an
occasional interruption. And calm-sounding, gentle number
two was always there. Now number two was number one and
always spoke of my unlimited nature.

The Process: Not Lengthy or Difficult

How long did this process take? I don't really know, but
it was a year and nine months or so before I could really rely
at all times on hearing my second voice (which was now
number one), a year after my European trip, and 21 months
after my decision to rely totally on my inner guide for all
decisions. The second voice—which I now call my inner
guide—just became more and more available to me. I enjoy
using it, and in doing so I also enjoy discovering all the wonderful places, people, and experiences to which it leads me.
Only my trust and faith in its guidance are required; no special exercise or conditions are necessary except opening my
mind and being willing and receptive.

Did I ever get lost? I really don't know. I know that I
would sometimes drive around a town or go places I had

never intended to go, but I always enjoyed myself. I never missed a ferry, lacked a good campsite, a hotel room, a restaurant, or anything. In fact, I camped in the rain on only two occasions, both times because I wanted to, not due to misdirection. In Europe, that's a miracle!

The Process: Not Fearful, But Unlimited

I was never bothered by anyone, although at times I was told by people that I was going to be, and I would ask for inner guidance. On each occasion, the person who seemed to threaten me in some way turned out to be helpful and friendly, often going beyond his or her personal comfort to assist me. I was led to experiences and places that would not have been open to me if I had been afraid. Picking up hitchhikers or accompanying people in strange circumstances was commonplace and only blessed me and heightened my enjoyment. At all times, I felt at ease and was never fearful. I did not see these experiences as tests, but rather as opportunities to participate in the local life fully with my newfound friends.

Inner Guide Never Tests Us

I do not recommend that you follow guidance that is

truly fearful for you. It is my experience that with inner guidance, the path is easy—not a sacrifice, testing ground, or a challenge.

I never considered myself in danger, and I was never asked to go someplace that would have made me really fearful. I always felt safe as a result of listening.

If I felt fearful (limited), I always asked for guidance and proceeded only when I was at peace. My inner guide (whom I regard as masculine) never tested me or pushed me into situations that caused me to worry. His guidance was always directed toward inner peace, certainty, and joy.

My First Voice Fades

Over this period of time, my first voice surfaced to a much lesser degree. Its rapid, fearful warnings and characteristically busy nature became easier to recognize. Its contrast with my calm, assuring, and friendly second voice had become very evident. I never felt that my true inner guide was forcing me to do anything. He was my friend, leading me to new and beautiful experiences. Things flowed when my friend was in charge, and I became more joyful and peaceful. That was the way I came to identify his presence within me—a feeling of joy and peace.

This is not to say that I am still not making judgments or that I am still not participating in the insanity of thinking that I can control what is going on. In time, these judgmental periods have become less frequent, have been of shorter duration, and their degree of intensity has lessened. They have become more obvious and ridiculous to me when I have participated in them.

I began to notice that I was enjoying many wonderful things. These experiences were quite beyond any events I had planned. Afterwards, I would look back on these instances with wonder at how well they had been handled, without any special effort or forethought on my part.

Our Inner Guide Can Help,
Even When We Don't Consciously Ask

Example

As I write, an instance in Rome comes to mind. I was in the downtown area, staying in a nice hotel near the train station. Since I had parked my car on the street, I was told by the hotel manager that thieves were prevalent in the area and, therefore, not to leave anything in my car—at least not in sight. While I had no fear that I would not be protected, I did follow his advice and put my bags in my room. As I ventured out to find a good restaurant, he also warned me about muggers and pickpockets.

Due to all these warnings, I was not entirely at ease that night as I walked the narrow, dark Roman streets to get a real Italian dinner. Yet I knew that I was not tempting fate and that I was safe. So, I proceeded in the moonless night. Instead of feeling threatened by the strange figures in the shadow-filled alleys, I decided to view the situation as a spy movie, and I was playing the James Bond role. It all seemed very funny, and it was in this mood that I looked forward to my walk home after a sumptuous dinner in a wonderful *ristorante* to which I had been guided.

Outside, I was accosted by a lady of negotiable affections. She whispered something in Italian about *amore,* and it took me a moment to comprehend the situation. Then it struck me that she was perfect for my "movie." She was in costume for her part. I couldn't help laughing as I put my hand on her shoulder and assured her I was not interested. She laughed, also, and for a moment we both played our parts, laughing together in the dark street about the silly plot. I have thought fondly of that laughter since then, and of how I truly loved her at that moment for showing me my "movie" and how little I had to fear. It was perfect. Each of us had spent our lives preparing for that moment, and it was very enjoyable, I am sure, for both of us.

Loving My Brothers and Sisters Is Natural

After I got back to my room, I reflected on what a wonderful encounter I had just had. The only loving response I could give that woman was joy and laughter. Judgment never crossed my mind.

"My gosh," I thought, "I am learning how to truly love my brothers and sisters. I don't even have to ask how to do it; it's natural when I am open and not fearful!"

Needless to say, I never lost anything in Rome or in any other place on the trip, and I was never cheated or taken advantage of in any way. In fact, the opposite was true. Time and time again, I received more than I gave. Gifts are still flowing to me from my friends abroad.

I want to restate here that often our inner guide speaks through sources outside ourselves. We can hear his voice from deep inside, but it may also come from our brothers, from books, art, music, or from anything we love or are willing to love. Love is the key.

A Course in Miracles *Is Helpful*

By the time I returned home to America, I was anxious to see how my newfound (but I suspected, old friend) inner guide would work there. After I initially got over the shock of it all—the size of the country, the big cars, and the hustle and bustle of life—I set about the task of devoting full efforts to improving my listening. I was finishing my first year's study of *A Course in Miracles*, and upon completion of the Workbook, I was proud to refer to myself as both student and teacher. This full awareness of an inner guide, referred to as Holy Spirit, or Voice for God, is the purpose for doing the 365 Workbook lessons. The final epilogue encourages students to "listen" to their inner guide as follows (pages 477-78 of the Workbook):

...He will direct your efforts, telling you exactly what to do, how to direct your mind, and when to come to Him in silence, asking for His sure direction and His certain Word. His is the Word that God has given you. His is the Word you chose to be your own.

And now I place you in His hands, to be His faithful followers, with Him as Guide through every difficulty and all pain that you may think is real. Nor will He give you pleasures that will pass away, for He gives only the eternal and the good. Let Him prepare you further. He has earned your trust by speaking daily to you of your Father and your brother and your Self. He will continue. Now you walk with Him, as certain as is He of where you go; as sure as He of how you should proceed; as confident as He is of the goal, and of your safe arrival in the end.

The end is certain, and the means as well. To this we say "Amen." You will be told exactly what God wills for you each time there is a choice to make. And He will speak for God and for your Self, thus making sure that hell will claim you not, and that each choice you make brings Heaven nearer to your reach. And so we walk with Him from this time on, and turn to Him for guidance and for peace and sure direction. Joy attends our way. For we go homeward to an open door which God has left unclosed to welcome us.

We trust our ways to Him and say "Amen." In peace we will continue in His way and trust all things to Him. In confidence we wait His answers, as we ask His Will in everything we do. He loves God's Son as we would love him. And He teaches us how to behold him through His eyes and love him as He does. You do not walk alone. God's angels hover near and all about. His Love surrounds you, and of this be sure; that I will never leave you comfortless.

Approachable by Many Means

Having completed the Workbook, for the next few months I attended several groups that were also studying *A Course in Miracles* material, and I saw that its study had many manifestations. Some *Course* students experienced contact with their inner guide by singing or by playing musical instruments, some through long periods of meditation, some through discussion and sharing, and some through more traditional reading and quiet study.

I could find my inner guide while running, sailing, or building, while meditating, or just by being quiet for a moment. I was growing to learn that I can have constant communication with this wonderful source.

The next chapter details the ten steps I was given through "inner listening." They can help you to find your own way. Be sure to ask your inner guide how best to listen, and then follow your own guidance. Each of us has his or her own path.

❖ ❖ ❖

CHAPTER 4

Ten Suggestions for Better "Listening"

"Inner listening" is our connection with the governing power of creation. I will use the word *God* for the sake of clarity. You may use other words if it pleases you, such as *principle, love, order,* or other cultural names for God. Our inner guide is our connection with God, and therefore, our connection with all knowledge, creativity, and harmony. How can we experience this "listening"? Here are ten suggestions:

1. We Need to Be Still

We need to still our minds, to let all thoughts but a desire to hear pass through our minds unresisted, to let go all our ideas of what we need, quiet our bodies' demands, and create a clean slate in our minds so that we can hear. It is helpful to put aside all concepts of who we are and what we believe— even such basic beliefs as what we call "good" or "bad."

We are created in spiritual harmony with the universe and are given a will of our own. A "foreign" will cannot be forced upon us unless we agree to accept it. Our minds are very powerful, and they create the world as we experience it. Willingness on our part, then, becomes the main condition we need in order to experience anything, including the ability to listen to our inner guide. Since our guide does not force us to comply, his voice is not loud and commanding. The voices of this world are conflicting noises that need to shriek and yell. They have no real power over us and operate only on the power we give them. They are based on fear, and like all bullies, they try to get their way by bluster and confusion. As we still our minds, we come into harmony with our inner guide's direction. We create a still, willing, receptive attitude that can be easily tuned to our highest good, eliminating all outside noise.

In order to hear properly, we must have the desire to change our *perception* of the world. This is quite different from a desire to change the world.

We must accept responsibility for our current perception

of the world as being the cause of our present experience and be willing to seek another way, to "listen" to another inter- pretation, and to see with new eyes. We have within us all that is necessary to do this, and it is available when we are will- ing to silence our other efforts.

2. Have No Investment in the Answer to the Question

"Listening" is difficult when we desire a special answer. We should realize that we do not know what is "best" for us, and accept what we are given. No one who already thinks he or she knows can truly ask. Many of our "questions" do not really seek answers. They are simply calls for justification of what we already believe. When we have already decided what the answer should be, how we will accept it, when it will occur, or how it is to affect us, we close our minds to receiving the "real" answer that is right for us.

We are like the child who asks, "When will you give me the ice cream cone so I can be happy?" We are really asking, "How soon will I get what I want, God?" If the answer is, "What you wish will hurt you," we refuse to listen.

Instead, we must say in our heart, "I willingly accept the answer given me as the truth, regardless of whether or not it pleases me right now."

We must mean this in our heart because all true questions are asked there. What our lips may say often means nothing, for our heart's desire is the true request. What we want in our heart takes precedence over all other types of requests.

3. "Listen" with Assurance

We are being directed even when we are unaware. We are where we are supposed to be and doing what we are supposed to be doing. God's will is not dependent upon our ability to hear.

We do not really need a clap of thunder, a holy feeling, a voice, or even a thought. Whatever is happening now is what is supposed to be happening, and is a blessing. Many of our queries are simply some form of the question, "Why is this happening to me?" This is our attempt to integrate what we see happening with what we think should be happening. We are heavily invested with death, sickness, bodies, and all the forms of this world. We have many judgments about what should happen and what we think would be best. These judgments are the result of how we perceive the world about us. They do not constitute reality, but rather, a desire to control our experiences.

We are spending time asking God to explain the insanity of the world that we ourselves create through our attitudes and beliefs. Then we ask Him to come into this insanity to correct our mistakes for us—not only to correct them, but to remove the consequences of our mistakes—allowing us to continue to make the same mistakes again and again, but without the usual painful results.

Our inner voice patiently explains this situation over and over by reassuring us that all is well—when we can see only chaos. It will eventually dawn on us that the only real request is, "Show us the blessing or the lesson You would have us learn." We then find that what was happening all along was for our happiness, and that we are being given chance after chance to learn our lessons.

Therefore, the question, "What is happening here?" if asked with a desire to change the situation and not to know what lesson is involved, will bring no useful answers. The ultimate answer to the question, "Why is this happening?" will always be, "Everything is fine, despite what we see, feel, or think about it, and despite what others tell us." God's will is always done, regardless of our awareness, or lack of awareness, of this reality.

4. God's Voice Is Everywhere

Since all things are echoes of God's Voice, be open to all sources. The truth will stay, and the rest will pass by. Songs, books, ideas, friends, and even "enemies" all speak for God's Love, so set aside time each day to listen and to write. Willingness is the only condition necessary for "listening." We can tune our awareness to messages from all sources.

This fourth point is a good one to spend some time on. The world tells us that we have to judge what comes into our consciousness; otherwise, we will get a babble of conflicting information. It is possible that this is not true. Robert Varley, at a conference in Palomar, California, in 1983, gave a moving talk one evening. He said he had thought for most of his life that he needed to screen out what came to him in order to separate the good from the bad. He stressed that when he finally began to question this belief, he decided to let everything come in and to have his inner guide do the judging. The result of this attitude is remarkable.

First, it eliminates our penchant for prejudgment and then puts judgment where it belongs—with our inner guide, and not with our five senses and past experiences.

It was Robert's experience that what was useful remained, and what was not useful just flowed by. This is a wonderful technique. For instance, we often judge what peo-

ple are thinking—when they have ideas that seem off base—
and especially when they hold a belief that we think is not
true since it differs from our own. We either wish to rush to
them to change their minds, or we dismiss them as not knowing what is going on.

If their idea is one that we believe will hurt others, and
we think there is a "better way," we feel compelled to use
almost any method short of violence to silence or change
them. Argument and ridicule are two techniques we often
enjoy using in these situations. We must admit, however, that
these practices seldom change another's mind, nor does
either person go away feeling more at peace or joyful as a
result of such an encounter.

When changing people does not succeed, we often use a
technique of ignoring them. This method, coupled with a
holier-than-thou attitude, is particularly satisfying for a while,
until we begin to notice that we are feeling very much alone,
ill at ease, and disturbed. Peace is not reached by promoting
conflict or by seeing others in need of being changed.

So what Robert Varley suggests is to allow all thoughts
to come into consciousness without any screening—to allow
them to pass through our minds without judgment, and to
identify with the person holding the thought and to love him
or her—for the person he or she truly is—regardless of
whether or not what this person is saying at the time is in

agreement with our own thinking and beliefs.

This technique works. Often we find that we are in much closer agreement with the person than we had originally thought. Our desire to love an "opponent" opens both his or her heart and ours. What is useful stays with both of us, and what is not simply melts away.

This does not mean that we have to accept all ideas and use them. It does mean that we do not stand at the door of our mind and open it only for what we judge to be right. We must stay inside the house, so to speak, and allow one wiser than we are to guard the door. Then all ideas that should come in do so, and those that do not belong go away, or they simply exit through the back door. We must, however, stand guard over our own thinking and encourage our mind to be loving, open, trusting, and honest. If we desire our thoughts to seek only the highest path, as directed by our inner guide, we do not have to worry about others. They have their guide, also, which comes from the same source as ours.

5. Accept the Answer—Be Patient

We may not get the answer we think we want, but it will be the right one. We need to be patient. The answer will come at the right time. We should not judge the message or the messenger. We should show that we accept the answer by act-ing on it. The answer is always a form of forgiveness for our-selves and for others.

We may not get the answer now because it is not time. Even if we feel we are ready for the answer, all the others who will participate in the event may not be in position. So we just wait. We must learn not only to ask what to do, but to ask when and how to do it. We cannot assume that the timing is now, just because we are ready. We cannot assume that we are to do something simply because we are aware of what is happening, or that something needs to be done. We need to ask and ask again until we are sure we are proceeding with love and guidance.

As we pose more and more questions to our inner guide, we realize eventually that we have fewer and fewer ques-tions. In the beginning, our question will usually be, "What should I do about this" and the answer is usually, "Nothing. It is being taken care of." We learn to ask, instead, "What is happening?" "What does this mean?" "What is the lesson here?" These questions allow us to be at peace.

We will become aware that at all times a plan is in action, and that this plan is for everyone's good. It is simply our inability to understand the plan and our part in it that caus-es us pain. By accepting the fact that we do not understand what is happening, and that whatever it entails is always for everyone's good, the only question we really have, then, is, "What is happening? Help me to see. I do not understand my lesson." This is our most honest request. Most of our other questions are obtuse attempts to get our inner guide to agree with our prejudgment, our plan, or our decision.

Knowing that all is planned only for our best interests, we can now turn our attention to everything around us and within us and hear what our inner guide is saying so we will understand. If we truly listen, we will discover that all life is sending the answer to us and is holding up placards, so to speak, saying, "This wonderful thing is happening! You are loved!"

This miracle is just for us, unless we are blind to it and do not look up. We can be so busy looking through our microscope to see the little separated details that we do not see the whole beautiful picture.

It would be very funny to see ourselves in a larger perspective...as a Mr. Magoo; and like the legendary cartoon character, to see that we have a guide who quietly removes all the obstacles from our path as we stumble forward through our nearsighted daily life, often unaware of what is truly happening around us.

Example

So what we must try to do now is be sensitive to all sources of information. A good example of this occurred when I took a mailer about my speaking engagements to my printer. I had spent lots of time writing down what I was hearing about listening, and I gave the mailer to the printer to set in type. As I read it, I made corrections and then realized that it was still wrong. I tried again and again to get it right and made several frustrating attempts. As each new sheet was set in type and thrown away, the cost soared. This was very frustrating to someone who wanted to lecture about "listening," and who could not even hear what the material in his own brochure should be.

Finally, the printer, who had read all my efforts but knew nothing about "listening" (I thought), looked at me with a smile and said, "Maybe you ought to try 'listening'."

"Damn," I said to myself, "who is he to tell me!?"

My inner voice then replied, "Who, indeed, but your dear brother with the truth?"

When I stopped and asked, with a desire to know what to do, I saw that I was writing about *how* I practiced "inner listening" and not what "inner listening" was about and how it affected my life. Once I was willing to truly "listen" with no investment, the material came. (Incidentally, it was printed just in time for a convention in Pasadena, where I had not known that I was going to be invited to speak until the day before the correct flyer was printed. I sent it out the next day as biographical data, since it was exactly what the convention management had requested.)

6. Only One Voice

The true inner voice is always known to those who desire the truth. It is the still, small voice that speaks of love and peace. There is no need to be confused about the illusion of numerous voices. We will recognize the truth because when we really know it, we are at peace.

So what can we conclude? The message is not determined by the form in which it comes. Since all worthwhile messages are of the spirit, their form is unimportant. This is contrary to the "world's" logical thinking again, which says that the form of the message determines its validity. Don't worry about the form, nor about the person who delivers it. The message can come from Willie Nelson in a song, "Live One Day at a Time," or from a 5-year-old child, a billboard, spiritual writings, the daily news, a politician, a priest, or our "best enemy."

If we are open, we will know when we hear the truth,

even if it is surrounded by all types of distractions.

No more needs to be said here. If we will think a moment, we will recognize the times we have felt this contact with the principles of harmony and love. We are at peace, with a sense that all is right with the world. Inner peace and joy are the guides to recognition of truth's presence (presents).

7. If in Doubt, Keep "Listening"

We will always know the truth when it comes to us deep inside. We will feel at peace and say, "Of course!" When we are confused, hurried, afraid, doubtful, or fearful, we need to keep "listening." All confusion is of our own making, and we merely need to let it go.

Once we recognize that we can hear clearly, we will find that life goes much more smoothly. We will get more and more reinforcement that what we are hearing is correct. All blocks to following this inner guidance will melt away. If the flow is temporarily interrupted, we simply silence ourselves, "listen" again, and we will be put back on track. (The feeling of "flowing in harmony" is, for me, a wonderful indication that I am "listening" to my inner guide.)

For a time, we may ask and ask again, "Is this the right decision?" or "Am I doing the right thing?"

We may not trust ourselves because many decisions we made in the past, which seemed right at the time, did not work out later. We need not experience this frustration when we truly "listen." Ease in "listening" and reinforcement of what we hear follows inner guidance, and we experience a sense that someone besides ourselves is making things happen. Miracles are the outcome of "inner listening." We do not arrange them, but we do experience them. They are the natural outcome of following our inner voice.

If we have "listened" without an investment in the answer and with no hidden plans, then what we hear will work and will bless everyone.

On the other hand, if we have heard with some investment (prejudice)—and we all do this from time to time—we will find that we simply need to "listen" again. Each time we make the new effort to "listen," we get a good look at what our investment is and at the lesson we need to learn. In this sense, the learning is to give up the investment—to let go of our judgment. We don't learn so we can *do* something better; we learn *not* to do something and to let go of what we are doing or think needs to be done!

8. Proceed If at Peace

We do not have to ask our guide for permission to do

everything. This speaks more of fear than of trust. We must have a desire to do God's Will and to be alert. We always need to ask, "What does this mean?" If our peace becomes disturbed, we should stop and ask for guidance and never force things. We should join our will with God's Will. This is letting go!

There is an old army command, "Proceed until further orders." We can use this in our daily life. If we make a habit of being alert to "listening," we will find that we can proceed without checking all the time and asking questions about every little thing. Our inner guide will alert us if something is off track. Until that time, an attitude of continual questioning may be just a lack of trust and a way of avoiding our own responsibility. We can always assume our inner guide is on duty and that things are going fine. If they are not okay (in the sense that they are out of harmony), we will know because we will not feel peace and joy. Then we can quickly rededicate our "listening." We can proceed with power and confidence, keeping our antennae raised for constant communication. Fear, uneasiness, pain, and slight irritation are all signs that it's time to stop and increase our listening.

We cannot go wrong by being willing to let the screening occur beyond our level of judgment and consciousness because we are protected by our guide. Even if we accept wrong ideas, they either seem to go nowhere or they become such a burden that we put them aside in the end. By letting our inner guide do the sorting out, we save time and enjoy the process more. This is the amazing part. "Listening," and being directed, is fun.

If we hear wrong, we still cannot miss. We will get there anyway. By not "listening," we just take the longer route.

Knowing this can help us to hear better because "listening" is taking the least painful road with the best view. If life becomes bumpy, it is a reminder that we got off at a wrong turn and that we can get back on the road just by stopping and checking inside with our guide, who has the only true map. Even when it seems impossible to get back, and things are confused, our guide is always there and will get through to us again when we are ready to listen and to follow his guidance.

Most of all, this realization helps us when we see others who we think need help. They seem to be unwilling to go inside to "listen" to their inner guide and to be at peace. But we should realize that they are only on temporary detours and that they will return to the high road when they are ready and willing. Remember, we all "listen" to some extent all the time. Those who seem to need our guidance really need our love, support, and encouragement. We should avoid the temptation to become their guide. That is not our job. They have their own guide, just as we do, who is waiting to help at all times and who also is aware of all circumstances and of what is really needed.

9. "Listen" for Reassurance

The purpose of "listening" is to have peace. We should "listen" to hear what is being done, not just to learn what we should be doing. If we are upset, it is because our perception is mistaken. All is well.

One of the members of our *Course in Miracles* group, Alma Copp, stated this thought in another way. She saw ideas as seeds. As seeds (ideas) fall to the ground, some spring up and are nurtured, while some do not grow. It is not our job to protect all seeds, but to nurture the young plants. Even the seeds that do not grow provide food for those that do.

I experienced this in creative, think-tank sessions at the advertising agency. As long as all ideas were accepted and built upon, the session continued, often generating lots of new and fresh ideas. But once we began to criticize certain thoughts, the entire supply of ideas dried up. The rule for these sessions was, "You can add to ideas or come up with new ones, but you can never criticize any idea offered."

Think of it this way: There is an unlimited source of ideas to meet all situations. When we are open, we take in all of the available ideas. After we have taken them in, the ones that will work start to grow and become apparent. The others may just rest there until needed later, or they may provide food for new ideas. If we sort out the ideas that are useful, or judge some good and some bad immediately, we may miss some and stop looking before we have found the proper solution.

The right answer is never forced upon us; it requires our willingness to want it. Then it is given to us, or, in reality, we become aware of it. We should not force ideas on others.

10. Daily Devotion

In order to hear properly, we must desire to change our perceptions of the world. We must accept responsibility for our present perceptions and be willing to see another way. A Course in Miracles *sets forth all that is necessary to accomplish this. Its aim is to make us aware of the guide and teacher we have with us always. However, it is important to pick the path that most appeals and speaks to you. You can "listen" to determine what this should be.*

It is helpful to set aside certain times during each day devoted just to the purpose of getting in touch with our inner guide. At least one-half hour each morning and evening is suggested. It is helpful to write down what we hear and to read it later. All efforts made in this regard will be rewarded.

We can share what we are told to share, but remember that the message or guidance we receive is primarily for us.

It is rare that we get messages for others from our inner guide.

We are to learn our lessons, follow what we hear, and then share our experiences with those who express a desire to hear. We are told when to share, and we are led to those who wish to learn. What we hear should not be used to teach others what we think they need to learn. Again, we must realize that each person has his or her own guide. (In reality, there is only one guide and one source, but it can be experienced in many forms.) When I am asked by others to "listen" for them, I am usually told by my inner guide to help them "listen" for themselves. We can join together as a group and intensify our ability to hear, but the messages we receive, even in groups, are still first for us. Joining in groups to listen can be a powerful tool and often provides a heightened sense of peace and well-being.

We should not attempt to use the messages we hear to attack others, or to force them to do things our way. That is never the purpose for which our guidance is received. The messages from our inner guide are always of love and support. To see another in need and to seek to cure that need— or to feel the desire to cure that need—is neither healing nor loving. Healing is of God, and we can share it by seeing our brothers and sisters as whole and complete, with all they need provided for them.

If we see another in need, we must ask our guide how to see that person differently, realizing that what we see in others we are also seeing in ourselves. If we are confused about how to be helpful, our guide will show the way and provide the proper opportunity.

✧ ✧ ✧

*In reality you are always guided
and cared for, remaining in constant
communication with your source of
knowledge, power, and harmony.
That is the true meaning and
expression of life.*

CHAPTER 5

Seeming Difficulties
in "Listening"

We will now discuss methods of resolving any seeming difficulties in "listening" that we may have. Often we want to "listen," but we cannot seem to hear. Even though we know that literally everyone and everything in our environment is trying to communicate with us, we still cannot hear. Why does this happen, and how do we get out of the trap? Believe it or not, it happens because we do not really want to "listen"!

On the surface, we may ask for guidance, but we often have the answer to our own question already formed, and so what we are really asking for is its affirmation.

This affirmation cannot be given to us if it is not the truth, and, therefore, not in our best interests. Thus, even when we do not seem to hear, we are being assured that we are still in communication. We are being given a silent "No!" Several things are happening.

Hidden, Preconceived Answers

If we are experiencing difficulty "listening," we should realize that we have hidden, preconceived answers to our "predicaments" that we have not yet uncovered and, therefore, are unwilling to let go and "listen."

We know, at a higher level, that these "answers" we are holding secret, even from ourselves, are incorrect; therefore, if we let them go we will be rejecting falsity and not truth. Our inner guide will gladly affirm any thoughts we have that are true because these are in concert with our highest mind. So, if we are not getting affirmation and feel confused, we know something we are holding on to needs to be corrected. Our highest self, or mind, is always in concert with God, the source of all knowledge. And since the two minds are really the same, such affirmations have great effect. We can ask that our hidden, preconceived solutions be revealed, and it will happen.

Our "Split Minds" Seem Real

This seeming "split-off" part of our mind, the part that seems out of contact with our Source—our highest mind or self—is the part that we often identify with. It has thoughts that it believes are apart from God—thoughts it thinks without Him. This "split mind," therefore, tries to hide these "split" thoughts, since it fears that it will be punished for having them because it knows its thoughts are in opposition to God. Guilt and fear cause some ideas and beliefs to seem to be forced below the conscious level where they are hidden away from us. When we are willing to seek out these "separated" thoughts and have them exposed, they will be brought to truth where they can be seen as illusions. Then they will return to the nothingness that they really are. So when we cannot hear our inner guide, we are believing that we are removed from God, the Source of all our knowing. We are believing that we can think apart, and are demonstrating our unwillingness to put our own efforts and solutions aside.

Where is a lie when the truth comes? Well, where are those millions who believed the world was flat, now that we have gone to the moon? The illusion is exposed, and it returns to whence it came: its basis—nothing. We are admonished by our guide not to try to reconcile truth with illusions. This is really what we do when we ask him to affirm our preconceived answers to our problems, and as a result, get silence.

For example, to try to prove the world is flat, we must believe false evidence. We cannot use truthful evidence to support this viewpoint, since no truth is there. The world is a sphere and nothing else; but until the illusion of flatness provided by our eyes is exposed, we can suffer great agony in trying to make the falsity fit. Anger, fear, and discord always attend the conflict as we try to defend falsity. Thus, the search for the truth may seem to be in conflict, but once truth is perceived, it is experienced as true inner peace. The false sense of "peace" accomplished by the acceptance of illusions is not true and lasting, although it may give temporary pleasure. The acceptance of illusions eventually brings fear and pain. The good news is that when we eventually reach the point where we have had enough of fear and pain, we will turn again to the truth. Truth is what is left when illusion is gone.

Truth and Illusion Seem to Be in Conflict

Truth does not cause conflict, since peace is one of its characteristics; illusions cause conflict, since they are incompatible with reality. Conflict will be experienced as long as we insist that illusions be maintained and supported.

We need not bring about truth through our own efforts, nor should we try. Truth, being a natural state, will exist for us when we no longer seek to support illusions. The earth is experienced as a sphere as soon as we do not believe it is flat. Letting go of the illusion of flatness, as evidenced by our eyes, allows us to conceive of the earth as a sphere. We do not have to pretend we see a spherical world with our eyes anymore. We need only change our minds about what our eyes see, and then we can know reality.

Thus, willingness to accept truth is all that is necessary for its revelation, experience, and eventual understanding.

A Short Period of Disorientation May Come

Our experience of the world comes from what we believe and seem to know. As we seek a different reality, an interim period of disorientation may occur. We are seeking something new, but we are still not yet willing to totally relinquish our old beliefs. Thus, we are tottering between two belief systems. So, as we devote ourselves to an intensified effort to "listen," we may feel increased confusion in our lives, which can be discouraging at the beginning. We should realize that the old judgments are being questioned and released, and we should have faith that seeking the truth will bring real peace in the end.

To illustrate, a dear friend was recently learning to ski. She found that in order to turn, she had to take her weight off one ski and transfer it to the other. In the process of weight transfer, there is a moment of imbalance. We must go through this period of imbalance each time we turn—whether we are skiing or switching from one thought system (fear and judgment) to another (love and trust). These periods of imbalance may be momentary or may last for a period of time. While they can produce discomfort, they are signs of real change.

This changing period may seem very strange. Disturbances seem to come at us from every side, drawing our attention away from the task at hand, as we seek a better guide than our own prejudices. We need to be diligent and watch the content of our minds. This churning, both inside and out, which may be experienced at the beginning, merely *seems* to be inconsistent with the goal of peace we want to achieve, but is *really* evidence of growth and progress.

As we commit ourselves to a single effort to follow our inner guide, a light will begin to dawn. At first, even in "listening," we have to set a single goal, and more than that, we have to work to achieve results. This "work" takes the form of more and more dedication to our single goal. As we progress, we can expand our uses of "listening" wider and wider, until our inner guide is used for all decisions and all judgments. The goal we desire is truth. The work is "willingness" to let go of all illusions. While it may seem to be "letting go," it is actually "receiving" peace as a final result.

The Tendency to Preplan

If our goal is to attain a close relationship with our guide and source, then the way will be shown to us. To decide on our own path, even in how to listen to our inner guide, is yet another method of determining in advance that we already know the solution to our problems. We can, and need to be able to, "listen" in all types of situations, but no special situation is necessary for God's voice to get through. Our willingness to hear is the only condition needed. If a special situation such as meditation helps, it is fine to use it, but do not rely on it totally.

Our willingness to hear need not consist of setting up special circumstances that we believe will increase or encourage our "listening." While special circumstances may be helpful on a temporary basis, we should be willing to let them go when they are no longer useful. Rituals are not part of inner listening. Form is not part of spirit in truth. We must be willing to let what is happening be the way we follow, and to be open to new directions. Following our happiness and inner peace will always place us on the proper path.

How clear! Whenever we make a conscious effort to set up a pathway to "get back home to God," we are trying to force our way instead of following our guide. Confusion and anger result. Anger, in whatever form—from discontent to rage—is a clear sign that we have a preplanned solution that is not working and that we need to "listen" again.

Willingness, therefore, needs to be transformed from a desire to follow our own path to a willingness to accept whatever direction comes—and to see it as a blessing.

To give up our own plan, considering the desire of most of us for organization and order, requires a great deal of willingness. We really cannot set growth criteria for ourselves, since we know neither the path nor the signposts along the way. If we preplan these criteria, then our past experiences, training, and beliefs will continue to lead us, and we will be sure to proceed in the wrong direction. What did not work in the past will not work now.

We must be truly willing to be as little children and see all things as new. We must ask our guide about everything and, as a little child, trust his guidance.

In following this childlike willingness—the most beautiful and difficult commitment—we place our faith in our inner guide and, in a real sense, take his hand along the homeward path!

HELPFUL HINTS FOR HAPPY LISTENING

Listening Has Many Joys

Just about everyone will eventually join in this great effort to follow his or her inner guide in all things. Through "listening," each one can tune in to one's own source of power and knowledge. To the extent that we make the effort, we will be rewarded. We may experience a voice, an inner knowing, or just peace. We may discover that things just seem to work out, from finding "unexpected" parking places to calling someone in need at the right time, or to getting a wonderful insight that results in a healing or change of mind. "Listening" can be used for anything from enjoying our work to finding peace and joy in our close personal relationships.

But "listening" will only be available to us to the extent that we are willing in our hearts to hear, and to the extent to which we are willing to give up our cherished expectations, thereby accepting what is given to us as a blessing and not a curse. This process is not of this world and, therefore, cannot really be explained in terms that this world will easily accept. Its best evidence is that "inner listening" works for those who use it. It is demonstrable, if not fully explainable.

A Course in Miracles *Is Helpful Training*

A few guidelines to listening are covered in this book. These are not complete and are to be used only to the extent that they are helpful. They are not mandatory, nor are they to be followed slavishly, but they are offered in the form of suggestions based on my personal experience and revelations.

Above all, as suggested earlier, one of the best sources for finding inner peace through listening is *A Course in Miracles*. These three books (also available in one volume), containing a year-long, self-taught course, are designed to assist in contacting our inner voice. They were "scribed" between 1965 and 1972 from an inner voice identified by the listener as Jesus the Christ, or Christ-consciousness, and they represent the most beautiful and helpful accounting of the truth I have ever found. They are recommended without any qualification and provide the basis of study followed very successfully by thousands of people.

Other Paths Are Also Helpful

However, the *Course in Miracles* books do not provide the only path, as they state themselves. Those who are currently on a path that is helpful are encouraged to continue with it. Each of us has an inner guide who is directing our footsteps now. Whether we hear correctly, well, or even faithfully, we are being led; we need have no concern about that. All that I can offer are my personal experiences, which may provide some clues and shortcuts for your journey. Each journey takes its own path, with its own turns. We should avoid the desire to force others to follow a special course in the name of truth and helpfulness. As each of us is ready, new avenues open, and new junctures bring new opportunities.

At each fork in the road of our inner journey, we can proceed with confidence that we cannot make the wrong choice if we are not doing the choosing alone, but are "listening" inside first.

A Course in Miracles stresses that the length of the journey is really an illusion; we are assured that the "journey" is over and done already. We need merely to awaken to our reality and to desire this awareness above all things. However, in this world of time, space, and form, we need to make an effort because we believe something needs to be done. All efforts to follow inner guidance are rewarded. We need to support any effort by others to follow a spiritual path, whether theirs agrees with ours or not. Once they are aware of "the path," they are then following inner guidance and are on the way.

New Vistas Open

The more I "listen" to inner guidance, the more clarity I get about the world around me. I do not so much hear what to *do,* as I hear how to *be.* A few years after my trip to Europe, I was asked to coordinate a Forgiveness Day Celebration by the Las Brisas Foundation. It was to be a fundraiser to help build our Retreat Center. When I asked my inner guide what to do, the instructions were to offer a half-hour appearance to everyone who wanted it. The schedule would be arranged by asking each person when they wanted to appear. This involved more than 16 time slots. Over the course of the next week, a number of people offered to appear and share their thoughts. It was amazing to watch all the slots being filled without any problem or conflict. I had only two people who wanted the same time slot. I asked my inner guide what to do and was told that all was well. Within a short time, one person called and said he could not make it. It is wonderful to be part of, and aware of, the Divine plan.

I was then told the morning of Forgiveness Day that I was to announce to those in attendance that anyone who wanted to appear and share should contact me. This really panicked me because I assumed that people would try to dominate the platform. However, I was assured that if I asked my inner guide about each request, all would be fine. Many people came up to ask to share, and some of the spontaneous sharing was very profound. It was all going very well until a group asked to have a one-and-a-half hour time slot. Not only that, but they needed a video set and a large screen. I now panicked. There was no space, all slots were taken, but as of yet I hadn't had to turn anyone away. I asked my inner guide and was told to offer the group the one-hour break for dinner. Another group that presented earlier offered them their video equipment to use. They were delighted, and it all worked out very nicely.

As I returned from dinner and the crowd started to file in, the "dinner" group on stage finished their presentation. Despite my fears and my feeling that this group would be disruptive, there was never a conflict. It was a magical day— one I will never forget. Everything went smoothly in spite of those times when I could see no solution to the problems. My inner guide was always able to work things out.

The next morning I was in a state of euphoria as I sat on my patio and looked out over the ocean. It was one of those days when time stands still, and I could easily see how perfect and harmonious the universe really is. It was so simple and well ordered, and each person, including me, was safe and loved. I cannot describe this spiritual awakening even though I have tried to remember it. It slowly slipped away, but I have had many others since them. They are always breathtaking and filled with wonder. As you continue to *"listen"* more and more, you will move into a place of peace that passes beyond your human awareness and understanding. You will come to realize that you really are unlimited.

❖   ❖   ❖

CHAPTER 6

Fifteen "Listening" Principles—A Checklist

H ere are some steps we can take to increase our ability to hear. They involve watching our mind work. We should check ourselves often to see if we are falling into any of these little traps:

1. Banish Preconceived Ideas—
Make a Clean Slate

Before we try to get in touch with our insight (our inner guide), we can make a concerted effort to put away any preconceived ideas about the answers to our questions, the direction we should take, or the choices we should make.

2. Monitor Our Thoughts for Grievances— Real or Perceived

We can practice watching our thoughts through the day, noticing how grievances pop up and are accepted quickly. We should make a point of putting them aside and being conscious of their effects upon our experiences. Grievances are efforts to put our own plans into effect, and then to judge others based on how they fit our plan. We must put those plans aside and follow our guide through inner listening in order to experience peace.

3. Accept Others—Learn to Trust

We can learn to trust others and to honor them, allowing our inner guide to be the judge of their ideas, actions, and appearances. Any of us can accomplish this, thus increasing our ability to hear our inner guide. We do not have to accept everyone's beliefs or ideas, but can simply allow them to flow through us and know that they cannot harm or affect us in any way unless we so choose. We will often find that ideas that are in conflict with our beliefs will melt away, even as those who express them soften before our eyes as we accept them without judging their beliefs, and as we show that we value them.

4. All Things Aid in Discovering Truth— Keep an Open Mind

A related idea is that everyone and all things can and do contribute to our discovery and awareness of the truth. Others we meet may be in contact with the truth in different ways, but this diversity can add dimensions to our own realization of truth, rather than providing conflict. Seldom can we perceive a situation in its entirety. Others can provide the benefit of new approaches that will expand our understanding and comprehension. We can grow in the realization that our identity is shared. Our true nature is oneness and connection, not individuality and separateness.

5. Keep Seeking—Don't Give Up

The solution to the question we are asking is always within the problem as well as within ourselves. We can learn not to seek the answer in other places. We need to stay with the alleged problem and wait for the answer to dawn upon our consciousness. Seeking, by dropping the problem and running away, will only bring us into contact with it later, on a larger scale.

For example, if someone is bothering us, we should not seek another who agrees with us in order to get a temporary sense of well-being. We should, instead, continue to go within for guidance until we have our peace by going past the supposed conflict with the person in question. This does not necessarily mean that we will ever agree with the other person, but it does mean that we will value his or her point of view and make our peace with this belief. This done, we will no longer be in conflict, but we will find that we have many areas of agreement.

It is not necessary, nor is it even beneficial, to force all conflicts into agreement. Often this requires denial, falsity, coercion, and compromise. The truth always comes to the front, and illusions always pass. Allow this to happen, and do not insist upon immediate solutions. We need to leave both the answer and the time of resolution to our inner guide.

6. Allow Ideas to Flow—Be a River

We can become a river and not a dam. By allowing all ideas to flow through us, we avoid creating stress. When we start to resist ideas, judge them, and then defend against them, we create a dam that builds pressure in our minds and stops the flow of all ideas. Again, we can be assured that those ideas that are beneficial will stay and grow within our consciousness, and all others will simply flow by without resistance. We should be discerning with respect to our own thoughts, yet not be judgmental of others' ideas.

7. Identify the Problem— Seek Deeply and Honestly

We should clearly identify our question or problem and be willing to be honest with ourselves so that all hidden resistance can be brought to the surface. Often we fail to get answers because we are unwilling to know what our real question is. To know requires that we be very honest with ourselves and that we truly seek to know—and not seek as a way to justify our current beliefs—most of which are capable of improvement. As a result, we should not get attached to any of them. We identify the problem to move past it, not to try to solve it on our own. The act of "solving problems" attempts to make them real; "going past them" returns them to their state of illusion. There are no problems. All is as it should be.

8. Do Not Rush the Answer—
Be Patient, Not a Patient

We need not rush the answer, for it will come at the right time for all concerned. Often we will find that we had the answer all along, but we either did not understand how to use it or we did not realize what the real question or problem was. So we were unaware of the answer. The real answer is, "There *is* no problem." We need to be gentle with ourselves and others. We're just fine, and so are they. Therefore, we can easily be patient, knowing who is in control.

9. The Answer Is for Us—Not Others

The true answer is not of us, but it does come through us. And the answer is for us only. Again, we must not get in the habit of asking on behalf of others. Ours is the mind that needs clarification, and it is in our own mind that the work must be done. Once we know this, knowledge may be shared as far as how we have learned to see differently, but not for the purpose of changing or affecting others. When we fall into the trap of seeing that others need to work on certain problems, we may be sure that *we* need to work on them, too! Seeking to project our problem onto the actions of others is a very old trick of our "split" minds. "The problem is not in our stars, but in ourselves." No one can really hurt us unless we allow our minds to accept attack. No one affects us unless we allow his or her beliefs or actions to do so.

Any perceived problem is always in our minds, no matter how much it seems to reside elsewhere with another's actions. When we are open to having our minds changed, we will be given the answer.

10. The Answer Will Come—You Can Be Sure

We can be confident that the answer will come. It *will* come. We *will* find it. It *has* come. It is impossible to *truly* seek God's help and not find it. Again, the truth cannot be denied except by that illusory part of our mind that does not want to accept it and that seeks another solution more to its liking. Our inner guide always knows what needs correcting, and he stands by to offer guidance 24 hours a day. He never closes.

11. The Real Goal Is Truth— Have No Other Goal

We must be clear about our goal and constantly ask our minds what our real goal is. What do we want to come out of this situation? Why do we seek this result? Does it have a basis in fear or in love? Can we accept what is happening as a blessing, or do we see it as a curse? The only worthwhile goal, no matter how it is stated, is truth. We *do* want the truth revealed, for only the truth will free us and give us real peace. Willingness for the truth to be is, as we have said, the only requirement for hearing.

12. Open-Mindedness Is the Key— Willingness Turns It On

We must be open. Open-mindedness is the key. We must open all channels on our "receivers," even to the thoughts that we think are foolish or useless. The answer is always coming to us in countless forms. We need not worry that we will not find it. It is here now, but we may not be ready to see it and to accept it. We also discover after a while that we have been given the answer in many forms. It will be repeated and repeated until it is clear, recognizable, and made our own.

13. Record Thoughts for Study

We should take time to write down the guidance we receive, even if we think it is just our own thoughts. When we read the material later, we will be surprised at the meaning-ful insights and content. It is helpful to set up a special time each day that is devoted just to "listening." This should not be the only time we "listen," but our daily devotion will be rewarded. We will find the truth if we really desire it. When we are comfortable with a special time, it may be helpful to extend it or lengthen it. Eventually, it will be possible to lis-ten in every situation all day long. In fact, this is natural, and we can become used to following this inner guidance at all times and in all things.

14. Rely on the Gift—It Belongs to Us

We can rely on this gift of guidance. The more we rely on it, the more it will be evident. Release of our desires, beliefs, and plans requires action. We should be still, "listen," and then act. Without action, listening becomes a game. Treated like a game, it becomes unreliable because we can only expe-rience what we truly believe. Our "fruits" demonstrate our beliefs.

15. Guidance Is Dependable—
We Have More Than We Use

The more we rely on this guidance, the easier it will come to us. I like to use "radical reliance"—totally depending on my guide for all things. But guidance should not be experienced as fearful or dangerous. Since what we are hearing does not always agree with the "world's" thinking, we need to proceed without "worldly" support.

Thus, many have dispensed with the need to wear a watch, to plan a day to any great extent, or to make preparations of any kind. We may have appointments, but we are not tied to them; we set them to accommodate others. Those people we are to meet, we will meet. Where we are to be, we will be. We cannot sit at home and test this theory, but if we proceed through the day as it feels comfortable and right, all is provided.

After all, we are tapping into the main channel of wisdom and knowledge for the whole of creation. This real, creative power of love and truth has no resistance and no competition. How could we not rely on it totally?

✧ ✧ ✧

CHAPTER 7

Is It Working?

Finally, How Do We Tell When It Is Working—
That We Have the Right Answer?

The "world's" thinking will not be in agreement with our inner guidance much of the time. We should not rely on "worldly" support as a guideline for success. So, we need to use new methods of judging results.

Here are some thoughts to enable us to tell when our "listening" is working:

1. We Will Have a Warm Glow

When we feel a "warm glow" about the answer, from the top of our heads to the tips of our toes, and we want to say, "Aha!"—that is a good sign. We recognize the truth deep down. Many times the answer is experienced as something we already know but which is now brought into focus. The feeling may also be of things falling into place. The answer that puts all the pieces together. The solution to the mystery. A feeling of harmony and order beyond material needs and evidence. A contact with the spirit beyond the form.

2. There Will Be No Pressure

When answers are accompanied by any feeling of hurry, anxiety, or pressure, we are not yet there. Strange as it may seem, the thing to do is to wait and listen further, not to rush around in panic trying to find out what to do, or to solve what "seems" to need solving. Reassurance, peace, and support are part of the answer. They attend its coming and its awareness. Time is not a factor, despite the "world's" belief to the contrary.

3. Everything Flows

After we get the answer, everything flows, and we will get assurance from other sources that what we have heard was right. People may call to confirm or to join in and, as we proceed, many reinforcements from songs, signs, and strangers may repeat what we have heard. Since reinforcement is unsought, the support makes us feel as if everything is joining with us in harmony. Do not seek this. It comes of itself. Resistance means we are not yet there; flow lets us know we are on track.

4. Others Will Agree

If the answer involves others, they will agree without pressure, at times going far beyond what we expect of them for assistance and support. If not, we must not push them. We will not have to "sell" our ideas, or work to get others to help or support—they will come forward and support naturally. If we are truly flowing with our inner guide, all that we need will be provided. It may not be what we think we need, but it will be what is needed. If this does not happen, we must wait for clarification. Answers, along with the means for solution, are all supplied by our inner guide.

5. Serendipity Occurs

The answers, guidance, or concepts we have heard through listening take on dimensions we never dreamed of. Other people add to them, and they grow on many levels and in many ways. The ideas bless everything that comes near, as they continue to grow and to expand, encompassing more and more. No one ever loses. Everyone gains from reality, if they so choose, and they can be aware of this.

6. Ideas Keep Returning

Even if we put aside the ideas we hear through listening, they keep coming back. In fact, when we are unsure of an answer, we can write it down and wait. If it is right, it will continue to come to us. Others may restate it to us or suggest we do it, and on and on. The truth does not need our defense, but our support of it blesses all, bringing everyone the fullest happiness and greatest joy. "Returning" is not an excuse for not acting on what we hear. But if we are unsure of direction, waiting works because the answers will continue to come until we are sure.

"Listening" and Blessing Are the Same

The most wonderful thing about "listening" is the blessings that flow from it. Whenever we "listen" and use what we receive, we will find blessings flowing far beyond anything we ever could have conceived without our inner guide.

Involvement in a program of "listening," for this reason alone, is beyond value. At first, we may see "listening" as a way to get answers to what is troubling us, and that we do so is fine. Next, we will listen because of the wonderful insights this experience gives us. Finally, we "listen" because it offers an unlimited path of peace and joy. The truth in all situations comes to bless us and others around us.

But far beyond all the other uses for "listening," the greatest of all is experiencing the blessings that flow from inner peace, happiness, and the awareness of our unlimited being.

❖ ❖ ❖

✧ A CLOSING NOTE ✧

By now I hope you have decided to try "listening" on a daily basis and are ready to enjoy the results of following your inner guidance. I'd like to close with a few comments about the use of the process.

"Listening" does not get me off the hook. I have to make the decision to follow this guidance. I don't recommend that anyone use "listening" as avoidance of his or her responsibility. When I "listen," I may get reassurance, and that is fine. At other times, I may feel guided to go places or to make commitments, totally on faith, according to what I have heard. Faith is involved because the physical evidence is contrary to what I'm hearing. However, at all times, when following my guide, I am peaceful, calm, and joyous inside. That is how I know I am in proper attunement.

I know deep within my being, beyond my own judgment, that I am on the proper course. At least I know what the next step is, and even if I do not understand the final outcome, that next step is certain. That step is all I have to know. At all times, when I "listen," I feel on some level that I am being asked to choose. That choice, when I truly analyze it, is between fear and love, trust and doubt, forgiveness and guilt, and limitation and limitlessness. It is always between my Higher Self (spiritual) and my ego self (material). If I am confused as to which direction leads to fear and which one leads to love, the choice always becomes clear by "listening."

The next step, however, is that I have to choose. Even when I do not have to do something, which is often, I still have to make a choice. Maybe a better word is *commitment*. It is this commitment that brings the results to me. I need do nothing except make my commitment, and that is everything.

A commitment requires faith, trust, and honest "listening." Choosing is my responsibility. I am not a robot, governed by a cosmic power—benign, good, or whatever. I am not being dragged through a maze of tests to see which lessons I will learn, then to be rewarded when I do well. No, indeed! I am a powerful, perfect Son of God. My will, the result of my own choice, nevertheless, is very powerful. It is the only force in all creation that can ever keep me away from the awareness of my Creator and from realization of my true identity. No guru, philosophy, cosmic plan, or other device will do the work for me. I, and I alone, must choose the high path or continue to delay my awareness of my true nature. Each decision I make is of the utmost importance. To place responsibility for this choice elsewhere, or to defer my decisions to some inner voice, by whatever name, is to avoid my only responsibility...to choose.

✧ ✧ ✧

✧ <u>EPILOGUE</u> ✧

An acknowledgment is proper to all the beautiful souls who have trod this path—so numerous that I could not name them, nor am I conscious of all their individual entities. They are legion: scribes, teachers, priests, writers, artists, composers, lovers, friends, and "enemies." My deepest thanks and gratitude go to all those who have "listened" to their inner guide and who have chosen the high path, paving the way for those of us who seek to follow. I may not always agree with your experiences or your symbols, but that is not important. What is important is your commitment to follow your inner guide, who will show you the way, the path of light.

Until we have a chance to join again...you and I, Dear Reader...

My love in faithful "listening" to His Voice.

— Lee Coit

✧ TEN TIPS FOR BETTER "LISTENING" ✧

*(In reality, you cannot help but listen to God's
Voice all the time.)*

1. **Be still.** You need to still your mind—to let go of all your thoughts except a desire to hear, and to let go of all your ideas of what you need. You need to quiet your body's demands and to create a clean slate in your mind so that you can hear. It is helpful to put aside all concepts of who you are and what you believe, even basic beliefs related to what you call "good" or "bad."

2. **Have no investments.** "Listening" is difficult when you desire a special answer to any question you may have. Realize that you do not know what is "best" for you, and accept what you will be given. No one can truly ask who already thinks he or she knows.

3. **"Listen" with assurance.** You are being directed even when you are unaware. You are where you are supposed to be, and you are doing what you are supposed to be doing. God's will is not dependent upon your ability to hear.

4. **God's Voice is everywhere**. Since all things are echoes of God's Voice, be open to all sources. The truth will stay, and the rest will pass by. Songs, books, ideas, friends, and even enemies all speak for God's love, so set aside time each day to "listen" and to write. Willingness is the only condition necessary for listening.

5. **Accept your answer.** You may not get the answer you want, but it will be the right one. Be patient. The answer will come at the right time. Do not judge the message or the messenger. Show that you accept the answer by acting on it. The answer is always a form of forgiveness for yourself and for others.

6. **Only one Voice.** God's Voice is always known to those who desire the truth. It is the Still, Small Voice that speaks of love and peace. There is no need to be confused about the illusion of numerous voices.

7. **If in doubt, keep "Listening."** You will always know the truth when it comes to you deep inside. You will feel at peace and say, "Of course!" When you are confused, hurried, afraid, doubtful, and fearful, keep "Listening." All confusion is of your own making and merely needs to be let go.

8. Proceed if at peace. You do not have to ask God for permission to do everything. This speaks more of fear than of trust. You must have a desire to do God's Will and to be alert. You always need to ask, "What does this mean?" If your peace becomes disturbed, stop and ask for guidance. Never force things. Join your will with God's Will.

9. "Listen" for reassurance. The purpose of "listening" is to have peace. "Listen" to hear what is being done, not what you should be doing. If you are upset, it is because your perception is mistaken. All is well.

10. Daily devotion. In order to hear properly, you must have the desire to change your perception of the world. You must accept responsibility for your present perceptions and be willing to see another way. Set aside a special time each day to reconnect with your Spiritual Source. This can be expanded upon as it is comfortable.

❖ ❖ ❖ ❖ ❖

✧ ABOUT THE AUTHOR ✧

Nearly 20 years ago, Lee Coit began a quest for answers to his pain and frustration. He decided to devote an entire year to this search, and as a result, he discovered an inner guidance system. Since that time he has followed this inner voice in making the important decisions in his life. This path has led to a peaceful and happy life, the writing of several books that have international distribution, and to giving lectures and workshops throughout the United States and Europe. For nearly ten years, he ran the Las Brisas Retreat Center. His dramatic change from a very busy advertising agency executive to a content and happy spiritual being gives hope to anyone who is seeking a better way to live.

Lee is available for lectures and seminars anywhere in the world and makes every effort to respond to all requests.

If you would like to attend a workshop, please send us your name. We will then notify you of the time and place where we will be lecturing. If you want to sponsor such an event, please let us know, as sponsorship is quite easy. When we have enough interest for several workshops in one part of the world, we plan a trip to that area. Of course, we will offer lectures and workshops for any size group. The workshop can be held in a home or a public facility. We are primarily interested in the desire of the attendees to increase their spiritual awareness; we are not concerned with numbers, revenues, or exposure.

We offer either one- or two-day sessions, and also longer workshops if there is a desire. If we are requested to make a special trip to an area, we ask that our travel expenses be covered in addition to the workshop fees. Please write for our complete brochure regarding sponsorship of an event if you are interested. We would be happy to discuss the matter with you. *We would love to come to your area sometime and share this wonderful process with you and your friends.*

ORDER DIRECT OR FROM YOUR BOOKSTORE

LISTENING - How to Increase Awareness of your Inner Guide This was Lee's first book written over 20 years ago and recently revised. It details how to access and follow Inner Guidance in a simple and easy to understand manner. Many examples are given of how this process works from Lee's personal experiences. 119 pages **Price $9.95**

ACCEPTING - How to Increase Your Awareness of Perfection In his second book Lee explains and demonstrates how to move beyond conflict and defensiveness and realize that everything has the possibility of containing a "blessing". The book details his life after a major shift in his priorities and viewpoint. 130 pages **Price $10.95**

BEING - How to increase Your Awareness of Oneness In the final book in this series Lee discusses how to live a life of "being" rather than "doing". He illustrates from personal examples how when we accept that all of creation is joined and inter-connected we are sustained fully in peace, joyfulness, and abundance. 142 pages **Price $11.95**

A COMPLETE PACKAGE OF 6 NINETY MINUTE AUDIO TAPES

LISTENING, ACCEPTING, AND BEING

These six tapes were recorded at the Edgar Cacye Foundation in Virginia Beach in 1994 over a period of several days. They are not duplications of the book's material but cover it in a different way. This is a wonderful collection for the person who wants to delve deeply into spiritual guidance as a way of living their life. Available only in a six packet holding case.

Price $59.95

(Shipping and Handling Add $1.50 for first item and 50 cents for each additional item please in same package.)

Personal Consultation, Workshops and Lectures:

Lee offers spiritual consultation on the phone or in person for $50.00 for a half hour session. Call to reserve a time at (805) 208-2805

Lee holds seminars in Ventura, CA when 6-10 people indicate an interest. The workshops last from Friday noon to Sunday afternoon. Participants furnish their own food and lodging. (We can help with suggestions) **Cost is $275.00**

Lee will travel to various locations to give workshops and lectures on request. He expects to have his expenses covered plus $50.00 per person for each 4 hour session. Minimum group is 10. The price of lectures varies with the situation. (The travel expenses can be shared) **Call for details, we try to accommodate all requests.**

Las Brisas Publishing P.O. Box 2987 Ventura, CA. 93002 Phone (805) 208-2805 e-mail Brisas@ix.netcom.com Check Web Site For Up To Date Information: Info@LeeCoit.Com

✦ **NOTES** ✦

❖ <u>NOTES</u> ❖

✦ **NOTES** ✦